Me and My Place in Space

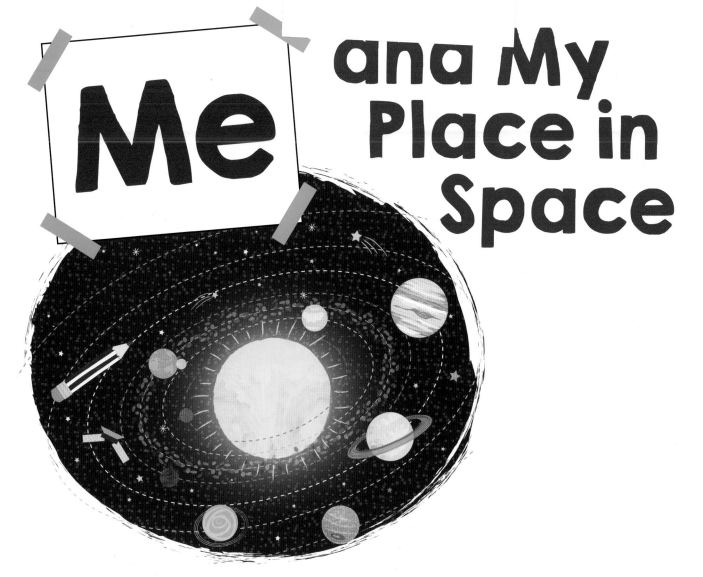

by Joan Sweeney · illustrated by Christine Gore

Alfred A. Knopf  New York

For the newest star in my universe, Keenan —J.S.

For Harry and Arthur,
I love you to the moon and back, x —C.G.

THIS IS A BORZOI BOOK PUBLISHED BY ALFRED A. KNOPF

Text copyright © 1998 by Joan Sweeney
Cover art and interior illustrations copyright © 2018 by Christine Gore

Visit us on the Web! rhcbooks.com

Educators and librarians, for a variety of teaching tools, visit us at RHTeachersLibrarians.com

The Library of Congress has cataloged the previous hardcover edition of this work as follows:
Sweeney, Joan, 1930–2017.
Me and my place in space / by Joan Sweeney ; illustrated by Annette Cable.
New York : Crown Publishers, c1998.
p. cm.
Summary: A child describes how the earth, sun, and planets are part of our solar system,
which is just one small part of the universe.
ISBN 978-0-517-70968-6 (trade) — ISBN 978-0-517-70969-4 (lib. bdg.)
[1. Astronomy—Juvenile literature. 2. Universe. 3. Solar system—Juvenile literature. 4. Solar system.] I. Cable, Annette, ill.
QB501.3 .S94 1998
520 97016169

ISBN 978-1-5247-7363-2 (trade) — ISBN 978-1-5247-7366-3 (pbk.) — ISBN 978-1-5247-7365-6 (ebook)

MANUFACTURED IN CHINA
September 2018
10 9 8 7 6 5 4 3 2 1
2018 Knopf Edition

This is me on my place in space—the planet Earth.

Tonight, I can see the Moon from my place in space.

The Moon is a ball of rock that travels in a path around the Earth, just like the Earth travels in a path around the Sun.

Earth

The Sun is a really fiery star,
as big as a million Earths.

Sun

So bright
and hot,
it lights
and heats . . .

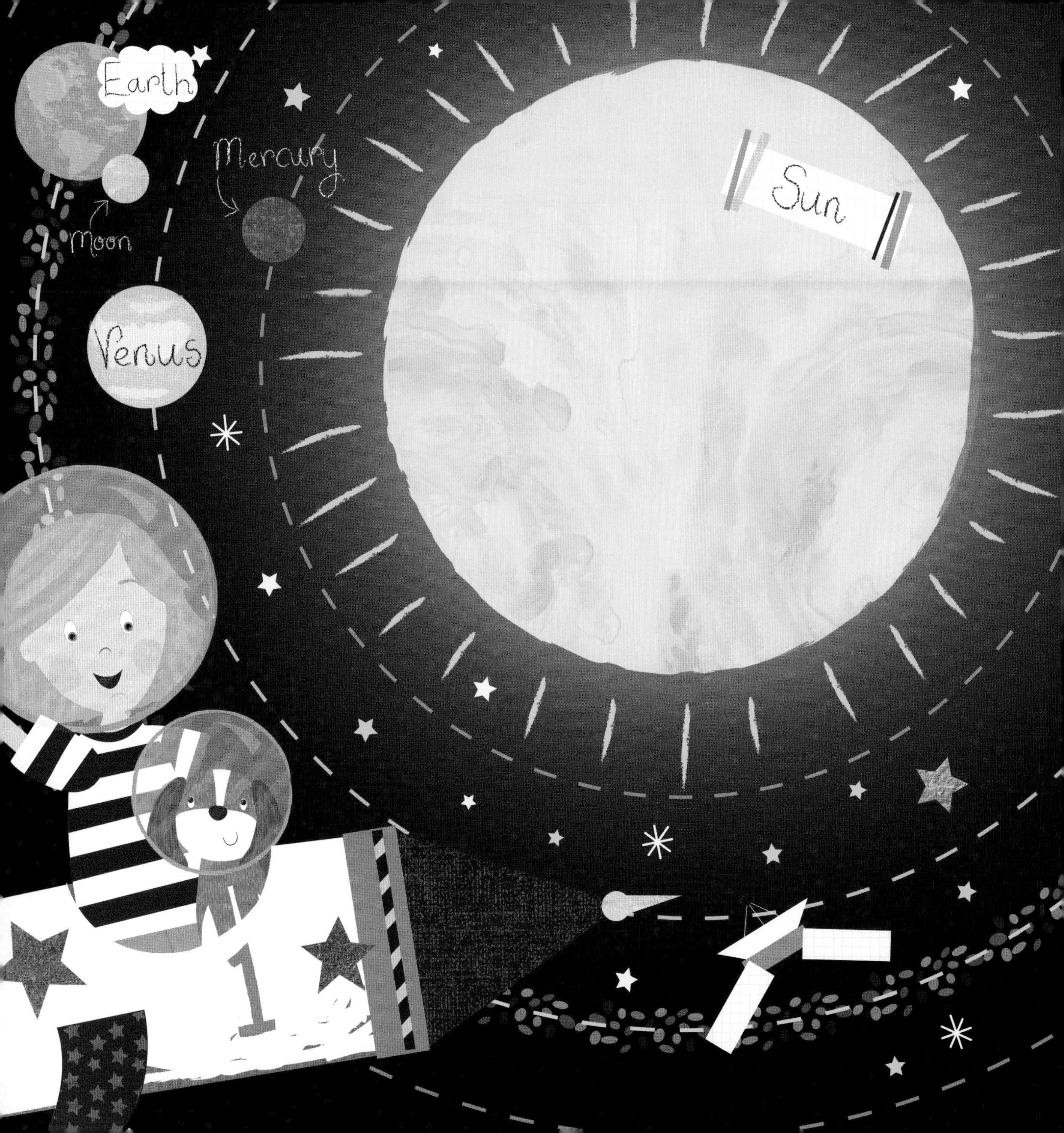
Earth
Mercury
Moon
Sun
Venus
1

On Mercury, the planet closest to the Sun, days are burning hot and nights are icy cold.

The Sun comes up in the west on Venus. Its gleaming cloud cover makes it the brightest planet of them all.

My place in space—beautiful
Earth—is the third planet from
the Sun. And the only one in
our solar system where living
things grow.

Long ago, there may have been life on Mars.
But now Mars is rusty, dusty, and cold.

Jupiter is a massive ball of gas, bigger than all the other planets *combined*.

MILES
AROUND

MERCURY
9,517

MARS
13,241

VENUS
23,615

EARTH
24,887

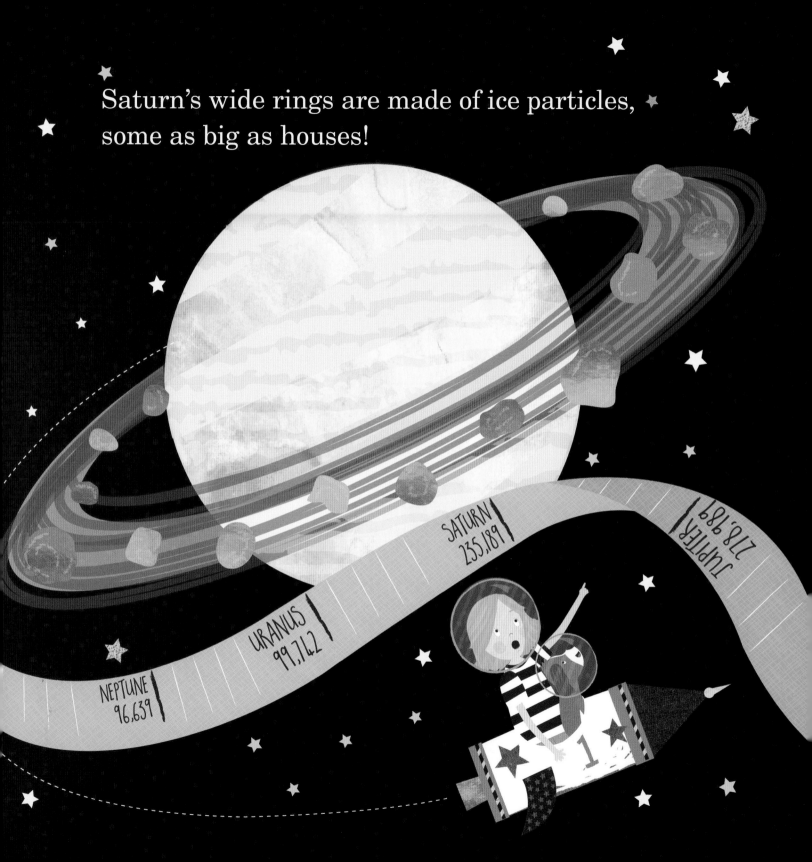

Saturn's wide rings are made of ice particles, some as big as houses!

NEPTUNE
96,639

URANUS
99,742

SATURN
235,189

JUPITER
278,989

On Uranus, it never gets warm, even though the Sun shines forty-two years in a row!

Neptune looks like a blue twin of Uranus; its Great Dark Spot is a giant cyclone, where winds blow at 700 miles an hour!

But as big as our solar system is, it is only one tiny part of the Milky Way—an immense galaxy made up of hundreds of billions of stars, some with solar systems of their own.

Our solar system is here!

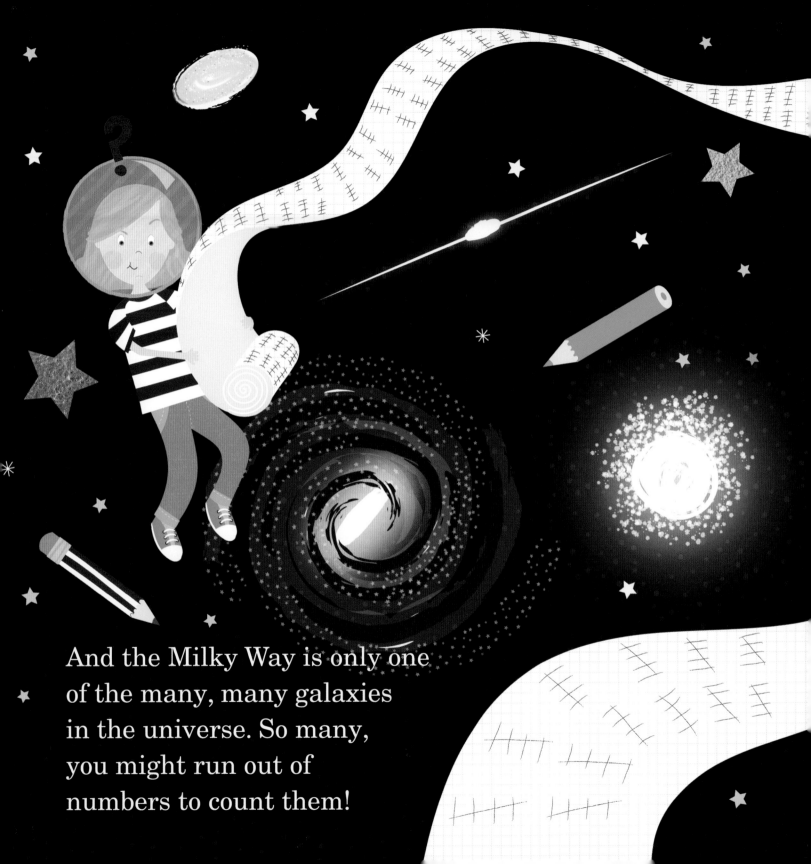

And the Milky Way is only one of the many, many galaxies in the universe. So many, you might run out of numbers to count them!

And the universe is *sooooo* gigantic, you could travel for trillions of years and never get to the other side.

Sometimes I wonder. Way out in space, is there another galaxy like mine?

Another solar
system like
mine?

Another Sun like mine?

Another planet like Earth?

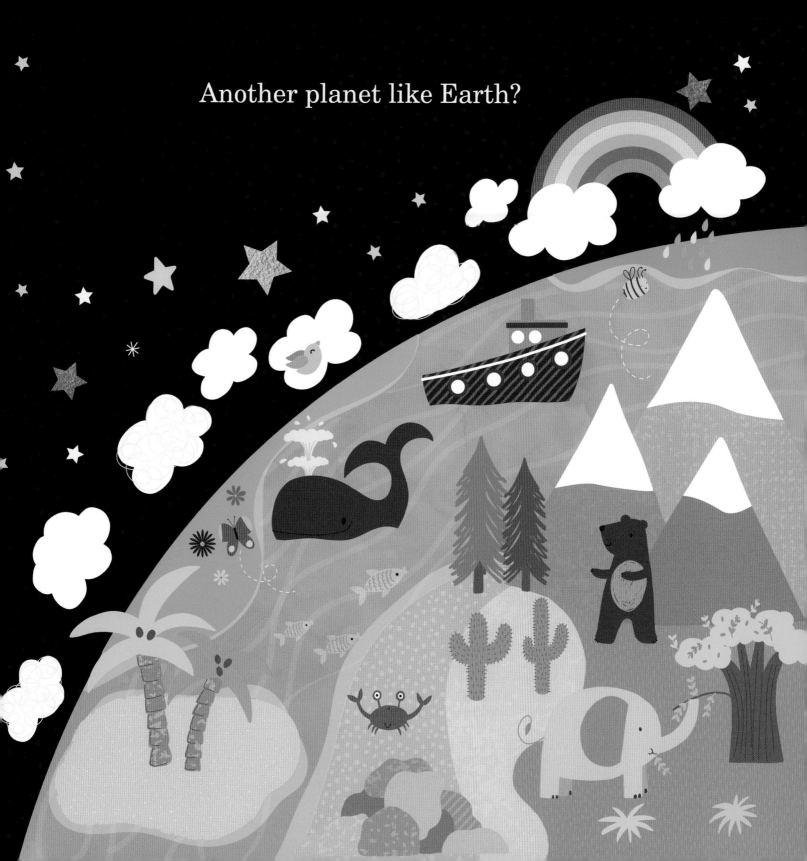

With another someone like me?

Saturn

The Sun

Could be.

Words to learn about Space

Galaxy: a group of many stars

Milky Way: the galaxy of which our solar system is a part

Moon: a ball of rock that moves around a planet

Planet: a ball of rock or gas that moves around a star

Pluto: a dwarf planet (Pluto was previously considered the ninth planet in our solar system.)

Solar System: a sun plus the planets that move around it

Star: an enormous ball of burning gas

Sun: a star that is at the center of a solar system

Universe: everything that exists in space